A Gift of

The Wellesley
Free Library
Centennial Fund

STATES

LOUISIANA

A MyReportLinks.com Book

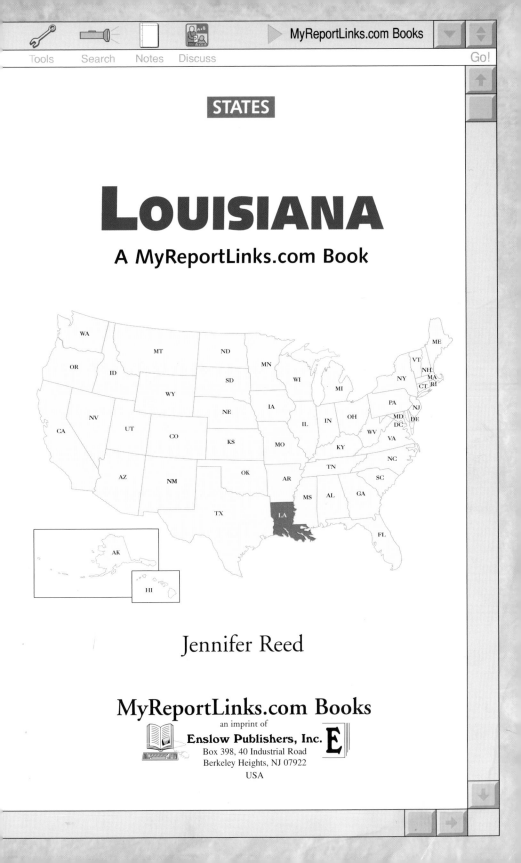

Jennifer Reed

MyReportLinks.com Books

an imprint of

Enslow Publishers, Inc. E

Box 398, 40 Industrial Road
Berkeley Heights, NJ 07922
USA

MyReportLinks.com Books, an imprint of Enslow Publishers, Inc. MyReportLinks is a trademark of Enslow Publishers, Inc.

Library of Congress Cataloging-in-Publication Data

Reed, Jennifer.
  Louisiana / Jennifer Reed.
    p. cm. — (States)
Summary: Discusses the land and climate, economy, government, and history of the state of Louisiana. Includes Internet links to Web sites.
Includes bibliographical references and index.
  ISBN 0-7660-5141-2
1. Louisiana—Juvenile literature. [1. Louisiana.] I. Title. II.
States (Series : Berkeley Heights, N.J.)
  F369.3 .R44 2003
  976.3—dc21
                                        2002153591

Printed in the United States of America

10 9 8 7 6 5 4 3 2 1

To Our Readers:
Through the purchase of this book, you and your library gain access to the Report Links that specifically back up this book.
The Publisher will provide access to the Report Links that back up this book and will keep these Report Links up to date on **www.myreportlinks.com** for three years from the book's first publication date.
We have done our best to make sure all Internet addresses in this book were active and appropriate when we went to press. However, the author and the Publisher have no control over, and assume no liability for, the material available on those Internet sites or on other Web sites they may link to.
The usage of the MyReportLinks.com Books Web site is subject to the terms and conditions stated on the Usage Policy Statement on **www.myreportlinks.com**.
A password may be required to access the Report Links that back up this book. The password is found on the bottom of page 4 of this book.
Any comments or suggestions can be sent by e-mail to comments@myreportlinks.com or to the address on the back cover.

Photo Credits: © 1999 Corbis Corporation, pp. 15, 20; © 2001, Robesus, Inc., p. 10 (flag); © Corel Corporation, pp. 3, 12, 25, 27; © EyeWire, p. 11; © Louisiana Office of Tourism, p. 22; © Photos.com, p. 31; © Tech4Learning, Inc., p. 23; AP/Wide World Photos, pp. 17, 30; Enslow Publishers, Inc., pp. 1, 10, 18; Library of Congress, pp. 28, 44; Louisiana Division of the Arts, p. 38; Louisiana Legislative Women's Caucus, p. 36; Louisiana Secretary of State, pp. 33, 35; Louisiana State Museum, p. 40; MyReportLinks.com Books, p. 4; New Orleans Tourism Marketing Corporation, p. 42; The Red Hot Jazz Archive, p. 16.

Cover Photo: © 1999 Corbis Corporation.

Cover Description: The French Quarter, New Orleans.

MyReportLinks.com Books

Contents

MyReportLinks.com Books
Great Books, Great Links, Great for Research!

MyReportLinks.com Books present the information you need to learn about your report subject. In addition, they show you where to go on the Internet for more information. The pre-evaluated Report Links that back up this book are kept up to date on **www.myreportlinks.com**. With the purchase of a MyReportLinks.com Books title, you and your library gain access to the Report Links that specifically back up that book. The Report Links save hours of research time and link to dozens—even hundreds—of Web sites, source documents, and photos related to your report topic.

Please see "To Our Readers" on the Copyright page for important information about this book, the MyReportLinks.com Books Web site, and the Report Links that back up this book.

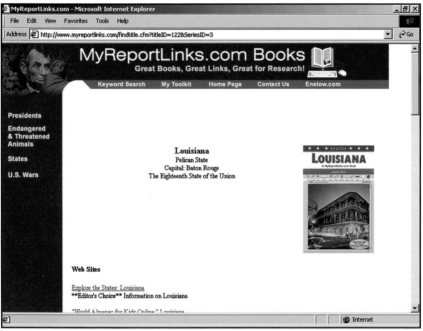

Access:

The Publisher will provide access to the Report Links that back up this book and will try to keep these Report Links up to date on our Web site for three years from the book's first publication date. Please enter **SLA1165** if asked for a password.

Report Links

The Internet sites described below can be accessed at
http://www.myreportlinks.com

*EDITOR'S CHOICE

▶ **Explore the States: Louisiana**
What does King Louis XIV have to do with the state of Louisiana?
Find out and learn more about the Pelican State at this site provided by
the Library of Congress.

Link to this Internet site from http://www.myreportlinks.com

*EDITOR'S CHOICE

▶ *World Almanac for Kids Online:* **Louisiana**
This site provides information about Louisiana's land and resources,
population, education and cultural activity, government and politics,
economy, and history.

Link to this Internet site from http://www.myreportlinks.com

*EDITOR'S CHOICE

▶ **The Secretary of State's Interesting Facts About Louisiana**
Louisiana's secretary of state provides information on symbols of the state,
including the state flag, the state bird, and the state musical instrument.

Link to this Internet site from http://www.myreportlinks.com

*EDITOR'S CHOICE

▶ **The Cabildo: Two Centuries of Louisiana History**
This detailed site from the Louisiana State Museum tells the history of
Louisiana from the time of its early inhabitants through Reconstruction
following the Civil War.

Link to this Internet site from http://www.myreportlinks.com

*EDITOR'S CHOICE

▶ **Stately Knowledge: Louisiana**
Read facts about the state of Louisiana, and view the state flag. See a
list of historical sites, major industries, bordering states, and more.

Link to this Internet site from http://www.myreportlinks.com

*EDITOR'S CHOICE

▶ **U.S. Census Bureau State & County QuickFacts: Louisiana**
This site, provided by the U.S. Census Bureau, gives us information about
the state of Louisiana. Included is information relating to population,
business, and geography. Comparisons are given to show changes from
previous years.

Link to this Internet site from http://www.myreportlinks.com

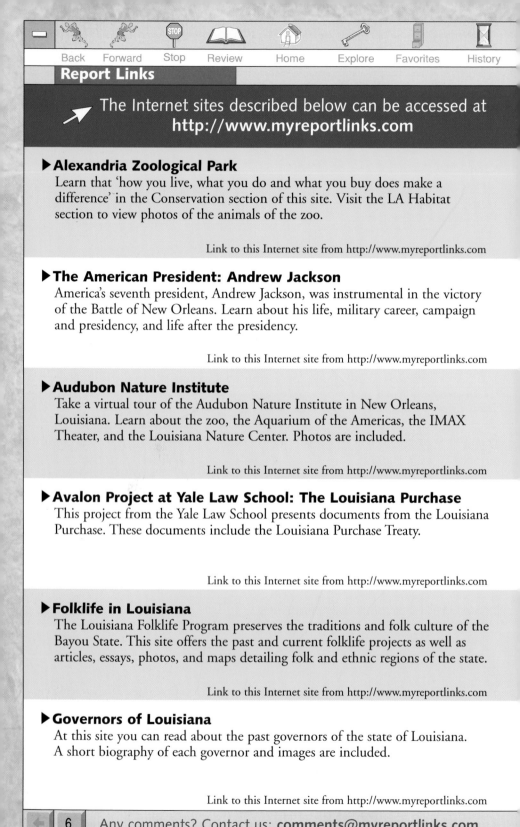

Report Links

➤ The Internet sites described below can be accessed at
http://www.myreportlinks.com

▶ Alexandria Zoological Park

Learn that 'how you live, what you do and what you buy does make a
difference' in the Conservation section of this site. Visit the LA Habitat
section to view photos of the animals of the zoo.

Link to this Internet site from http://www.myreportlinks.com

▶ The American President: Andrew Jackson

America's seventh president, Andrew Jackson, was instrumental in the victory
of the Battle of New Orleans. Learn about his life, military career, campaign
and presidency, and life after the presidency.

Link to this Internet site from http://www.myreportlinks.com

▶ Audubon Nature Institute

Take a virtual tour of the Audubon Nature Institute in New Orleans,
Louisiana. Learn about the zoo, the Aquarium of the Americas, the IMAX
Theater, and the Louisiana Nature Center. Photos are included.

Link to this Internet site from http://www.myreportlinks.com

▶ Avalon Project at Yale Law School: The Louisiana Purchase

This project from the Yale Law School presents documents from the Louisiana
Purchase. These documents include the Louisiana Purchase Treaty.

Link to this Internet site from http://www.myreportlinks.com

▶ Folklife in Louisiana

The Louisiana Folklife Program preserves the traditions and folk culture of the
Bayou State. This site offers the past and current folklife projects as well as
articles, essays, photos, and maps detailing folk and ethnic regions of the state.

Link to this Internet site from http://www.myreportlinks.com

▶ Governors of Louisiana

At this site you can read about the past governors of the state of Louisiana.
A short biography of each governor and images are included.

Link to this Internet site from http://www.myreportlinks.com

Report Links

The Internet sites described below can be accessed at
http://www.myreportlinks.com

▶ **InfoLouisiana**

This state site presents information on Louisiana's government,
population, business, tourism, education, and more.

Link to this Internet site from http://www.myreportlinks.com

▶ **Infoplease: Louisiana**

At this site you can read a brief history of Louisiana. Also learn about
the state capital and nickname, famous Louisianans, and more.

Link to this Internet site from http://www.myreportlinks.com

▶ **Long, Huey Pierce**

Read a brief biography of the most famous governor of Louisiana.

Link to this Internet site from http://www.myreportlinks.com

▶ **Louis "Satchmo" Armstrong (1901–1971)**

Read the biography of jazz legend and Louisiana native Louis
"Satchmo" Armstrong. Considered the greatest cornet player of all
time, Armstrong's career spanned decades. View a discography of both
his band days and solo career. Photos included.

Link to this Internet site from http://www.myreportlinks.com

▶ **Louisiana Fast Facts and Trivia**

Where did the name Louisiana come from? What city is "the Frog Capital
of the World?" Find out these and forty-eight other facts at this site.

Link to this Internet site from http://www.myreportlinks.com

▶ **Louisiana Folklife Center**

Read short biographies of Hall of Master Folk Artist inductees. This
hall includes wood crafters, storytellers, musicians, singers, songwriters,
basket makers, needle crafters, and historians. Links to other resources
are available.

Link to this Internet site from http://www.myreportlinks.com

The Internet sites described below can be accessed at
http://www.myreportlinks.com

▶ Louisiana Images and Guide
You will find "all things Louisiana" at this site. View photos of plantation
houses and churches that reflect the Old South. Learn about cemeteries that
are unique to Louisiana because of the high water table.

Link to this Internet site from http://www.myreportlinks.com

▶ Louisiana Leaders: Notable Women in History
The Louisiana State University library brings us this presentation of notable
women in Louisiana history, including Carolyn E. Merrick, Elizabeth Lyle
Saxon, Dr. Elizabeth Cohen, and Sophie Belle Wright.

Link to this Internet site from http://www.myreportlinks.com

▶ Louisiana Office of Tourism
The Louisiana Office of Tourism has provided a Web site with things to do and
places to see in the state. You will also find historical and cultural information.

Link to this Internet site from http://www.myreportlinks.com

▶ Louisiana Public Broadcasting: Swapping Stories
Storytelling is an art form in Louisiana. Enjoy these folktales as told by natives
of the state. Included are animal and magic tales, jokes, and tall tales.

Link to this Internet site from http://www.myreportlinks.com

▶ Louisiana State Museum
This site offers several online exhibits, including "Mardi Gras in La.,"
"Louisiana and the Mighty Mississippi," and "Louisiana Aviation Since 1910."

Link to this Internet site from http://www.myreportlinks.com

▶ Louisiana Supreme Court
Read about the Louisiana Supreme Court on this site. You can find out
about the history of the court system and read biographies of the seven
current justices.

Link to this Internet site from http://www.myreportlinks.com

Report Links

The Internet sites described below can be accessed at
http://www.myreportlinks.com

▶**Mardi Gras**
Find out what *Mardi Gras* means and the type of celebrations that take
place during this holiday.

Link to this Internet site from http://www.myreportlinks.com

▶**New Orleans: Lake Pontchartrain**
Read the history of Louisiana's Lake Pontchartrain. This site includes a
history of the lake, including the creation of the world's longest over-
water bridge. Photos are included.

Link to this Internet site from http://www.myreportlinks.com

▶**New Orleans Museum of Art**
The New Orleans Museum of Art has several collections for viewing
online. One of the museum's permanent exhibits is Louisiana Art, where
nineteenth century, twentieth century, and contemporary Louisianan
artwork is on display.

Link to this Internet site from http://www.myreportlinks.com

▶**New Orleans Online**
At this site you can learn about the history and heritage of New Orleans
as well as get information on things to do if you are planning a visit.
Be sure to take the virtual tour of New Orleans.

Link to this Internet site from http://www.myreportlinks.com

▶**New Orleans Public Library: African American Resources**
Presented by the New Orleans Public Library, this site features various
resources relating to African Americans, focusing on those in Louisiana
history. Also included are recommended reading lists.

Link to this Internet site from http://www.myreportlinks.com

▶**Welcome to the Louisiana Sports Hall of Fame**
At the Louisiana Sports Hall of Fame you can read a short biography
of all of the members. Learn about the history of the hall of fame.
Photos are included.

Link to this Internet site from http://www.myreportlinks.com

▶ **Gained Statehood**
April 30, 1812, the eighteenth state

▶ **Capital**
Baton Rouge

▶ **Parishes (Counties)**
64

▶ **Motto**
"Union, Justice, and Confidence"

▶ **Population**
4,468,976*

▶ **Nicknames**
Pelican State, Creole State

▶ **Tree**
Bald cypress

▶ **Flower**
Magnolia

▶ **Bird**
Eastern brown pelican

▶ **Insect**
Honeybee

▶ **Fossil**
Petrified palmwood

▶ **Reptile**
Alligator

▶ **Gemstone**
Agate

▶ **Songs**
"Give Me Louisiana" (written by Doralise Fontane, arranged by Dr. John Croom);
"You Are My Sunshine" (words and music by Jimmie Davis and Charles Mitchell)

▶ **Flag**
Adopted in 1912, the flag design consists of pelican and chicks from the state seal, in white and gold, and a white ribbon bearing the state motto, "Union, Justice, and Confidence."

Population reflects the 2000 census.

The Pelican State

Louisiana is a state known for its mix of cultures, its music, and its seafood. Louisiana is also known for being one of the wettest states in America. It receives on average fifty-seven inches of rain a year. Despite the wet weather, many tourists still visit Louisiana each year. The unique blend of French and African-American cultures was prominent hundreds of years ago and still plays a huge role in daily life.

Louisiana's population exceeds 4.5 million. People in the state tend to stay close to large cities and towns. However, many residents live in rural areas.

▲ New Orleans, located on the Mississippi River, is the largest city in Louisiana. Although this city is rich in culture and history, it is perhaps best known for its week-long Mardi Gras celebration held every spring.

▶ Louisiana's Natural Resources

One of the world's longest rivers flows through Louisiana. It is the Mississippi River—the longest river in North America. This river carves out the border between Louisiana and the state of Mississippi. About halfway down, the Mississippi flows through the state, no longer acting as the border. Then it empties into the Gulf of Mexico, carrying sediment the river has picked up along the way. This area is called the delta and makes up about one fourth of the state's total landmass.

The Louisiana coastline is in danger. Each year, waves and storms wash away sand and sediment that otherwise would add to the total landmass of the state. Louisianans have built levees along the river to keep it from flooding. A levee is a ridge that prevents water from spilling over. It can be man-made or natural. Some of the state's farmland is located near the levees. These levees also keep the sediment from traveling downriver and being deposited in the Mississippi Delta.[1]

▽ *American alligators live in the freshwater lakes, marshlands, swamps, and rivers of the southeastern United States, including Louisiana. The state has long been a leading producer of alligator hides.*

Lake Pontchartrain is the state's largest lake. There are many saltwater and freshwater lakes throughout Louisiana as well as slow-moving rivers called bayous. Bayous are located in the Mississippi Delta and make a great home for plants and animals. Nearly half the state is forested, and the trees found in these forests include magnolia, pine, and hickory. Animals found in Louisiana include deer, minks, raccoons, opossums, wild hogs, and muskrats.

Many animals dwell in the wetlands, swamps, and marshes. Alligators live there too. There are approximately 150,000 alligators in Louisiana, and the state is home to the only known white alligators in the world. Birds also thrive in the Louisiana wetlands, where bald eagles, herons, and brown pelicans can be found. The brown pelican is Louisiana's state bird. Many bird species are protected in Louisiana's state parks and refuges. The wetlands are considered the state's most valuable natural resource, and most fragile. With the constant erosion that occurs, Louisiana loses twenty-five to thirty-five square miles of wetlands each year. The state and environmental groups are ambitiously working to save the wetlands and the wildlife that lives there.

A Mix of People

Gumbo, a souplike dish made with a combination of vegetables and meat or seafood, is a Louisiana favorite to cook and eat. In a way, gumbo represents the many different cultures and ethnic groups who have come to live in Louisiana over the years.

American Indians inhabited the Louisiana area for thousands of years. Remains of ancient villages have been found throughout the state. Tribes including the

Natchez, Chitimacha, and the Atakapa hunted and fished in Louisiana.

As Europeans sailed the seas to find land and gold, the inevitable came upon the Louisiana Territory. As early as 1541, Spanish explorers, including Hernando de Soto, led soldiers, slaves, and missionaries through the northern part of Louisiana. De Soto was the first European explorer to enter the area.

Europe was not much interested in the land and it was not until a hundred years later that the French claimed the Mississippi Valley. Explorer René-Robert Cavelier, Sieur de La Salle, claimed the land, and in honor of the French king Louis XIV, named it *Louisiana*. Still not many people cared to live in Louisiana. In parts of Europe, prisoners were given a choice, "Death or Louisiana." Of course, many chose to come to Louisiana.

By the mid 1700s, Germans, French, and other Europeans were making their way to the New World and to Louisiana in particular. In 1763, the Treaty of Paris ended the French and Indian War (also known as the Seven Years War). England remained in control of Canada; France had lost its battle to control Canada. Thousands of French Canadians known as Acadians fled their homes. They moved to Louisiana, which at the time was under French rule, and settled in Lafayette Parish. Today their descendants are called Cajuns.

For the next fifty years, the territory of Louisiana would change hands from France to Spain and back to France. A great mass of land including a portion of the Louisiana Territory was bought during the Thomas Jefferson presidency for $15 million. This was called the Louisiana Purchase. French emperor Napoléon Bonaparte sold the land to the United States in 1803. Then in 1812,

One of the most famous landmarks of New Orleans is the Cathedral of Saint Louis King of France, which was established as a parish in 1720 when the city was under French rule.

Louisiana became the eighteenth state in the Union, the United States of America.

Many of the ancestors of the early French Canadians (Cajuns) and French, Spanish, American Indians, and Africans (Creoles) still live in Louisiana. They continue to speak French and maintain the traditions and culture of their ancestors.

Louisiana has inspired many people in different ways. Jazz and blues music originated here. The diverse cultures contribute to the many types of foods found throughout the state and the writings about Louisiana.

The Spice of Life

Dozens of movies and documentaries have been filmed in Louisiana. Beautiful plantations, the Mississippi River, and entertaining cities provide the perfect backdrop. Art has also provided an outlet for Louisianans, such as

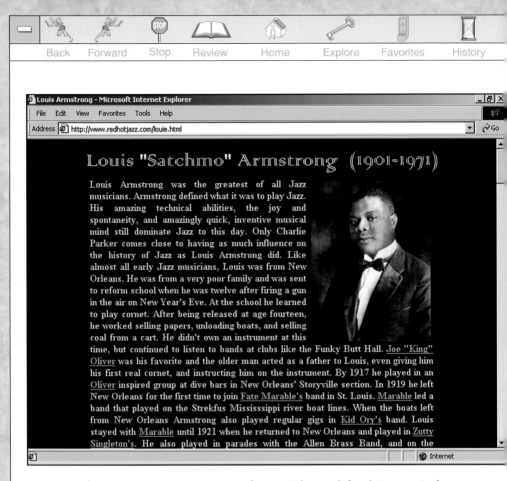

A Louis Armstrong, a native of New Orleans, defined jazz music for the world.

Clementine Hunter. When she was in her fifties, she decided to take up painting and became well known for her portraits. Painter John James Audubon worked in Louisiana for many years and published his most famous book, *Birds of America*, in 1838. The first artist to show his work in Louisiana was A. De Batz in 1732. He painted pictures of American Indians.

Authors also find inspiration. In 1764, colonists wrote about Louisiana and had their writings printed in France. Many books were printed in French, including *Les Cenelles*. This was a collection of love songs written by

African Americans living in Louisiana. Samuel Clemens, also known as Mark Twain, wrote extensively about life on the Mississippi and accounts of his trips to New Orleans. Other well-known writers inspired by Louisiana include Truman Capote and children's author William Joyce.

Louisiana, home of jazz and blues, has been home to some of the best jazz players in the world. The list of famous musicians includes Louis Armstrong, Fats Domino, and Harry Connick, Jr. Connick has been able to bridge a gap between jazz and mainstream pop music, showing that anyone can enjoy jazz and blues. Other well-known musicians from Louisiana are Jerry Lee Lewis, Aaron Neville, and Wynton Marsalis.

Louisianans are proud of their state and all it has to offer. Rich traditions, festivals, and a culture unlike any other in the United States make Louisiana not only a fun place to visit but also a great place to live.

Antoine "Fats" Domino was born in New Orleans in 1928. By age ten, he had learned to sing and play the piano. In the 1940s and 1950s, he used these talents to outsell every rock and roll record except those of Elvis Presley.

Land and Climate

Louisiana is bordered by three states: Mississippi, Arkansas, and Texas. The fourth border is the Gulf of Mexico. Louisiana is the thirty-first largest state in the United States. Water and waterways including the Mississippi River play an important role in both Louisiana's economy and culture. New Orleans, which lies eight feet below sea level, is one of the lowest points in the United States. Levees hold back the waters of the

▲ A map of Louisiana.

Mississippi River, which brings silt downriver. The river is fifteen feet above sea level. How can the river be higher than the city? The silt has built up over many centuries, causing the sides of the river to rise higher than the land.

Wet and Wild

Louisiana has two distinctly different climates. The northern half of the state has a moderate climate while the southern half is semitropical. This state is known for its hot and humid summers and cool winters. Summers in Louisiana are not very comfortable. The average temperature in July, the hottest month, is 82°F, but it is the humidity that often makes it unbearable to be outside.

Louisiana winters are comfortable, and snow is rare. The average temperature in January, the coldest month, is 50°F. The state's rain is brought in from the Gulf Coast.

The Louisiana coastline has been hit by many tropical storms and hurricanes. As cool air reaches the warm, steamy air over the waters in the Atlantic Ocean and Gulf of Mexico, tropical storms develop, which can also turn into deadly hurricanes. Hurricane Audrey was one of the worst storms ever to hit Louisiana. It hit in late June 1957, and took 390 lives.[1] Every year, when hurricane season arrives, residents of Louisiana watch the weather carefully. Chances are very high that a hurricane will find landfall in Louisiana.

The Three Regions

The three varied regions in Louisiana from east to west are the East Gulf Coastal Plain, the Mississippi Alluvial Plain, and the West Gulf Coastal Plain. The East Gulf Coastal Plain is all land east of the Mississippi River and north of Lake Pontchartrain. This area is similar to the western part of Louisiana with its steep bluffs in the Tunica Hills. Pine forests and clear springs can be found in this region.

The Mississippi Alluvial Plain runs along the lower Mississippi River from the Arkansas border all the way down to the Gulf of Mexico. The Mississippi Delta is located here as well and covers 13,000 square miles. This is the land of bayous, areas where the water of the Mississippi River has overflowed and formed slow-moving streams. Locals refer to this swampy, lowland region as the "Delta" though it does not refer to just the delta of the Mississippi.

The West Gulf Coastal Plain is all of the land west of the Mississippi Alluvial Plain. This area has hilly regions with bluffs often reaching three hundred feet. Mount Driskill, the highest point in the state, and the Kisatchie

▲ Bourbon Street, in New Orleans. The city's location on the Mississippi River has helped to make it one of the most important ports and one of the largest ports in the country.

Hills are located here as well as Louisiana's only national forest. The northern part of this region has rolling hills, and much of it is woodland. To the south, prairies and grasslands spread in all directions, while marshlands are found near the coast.

Water, Water Everywhere

Louisiana's coastline is being eroded constantly, losing between twenty-five and thirty-five square miles yearly.[2] The coastal marshes play a very important role. They are home to wildlife such as ducks and geese. Some species of plants that are not found anywhere else grow here, too. The coastal marshes protect towns located farther inland. The marshes slow down strong winds and hold in water when a storm blows through. Although the lapping waves of the ocean contribute to the eroding coastline, the Mississippi River carries silt and soil downstream and deposits it back into the marshes. Over time, people have built so many levees to protect themselves from flooding that they have straightened out the river in some places, causing the river to flow faster. The silt and soil that once replenished the coastline is now carried straight out to sea.

Mining is also increasing the speed of coastal erosion. Oil and natural gas are found in the coastal marshes. In order to get these needed natural resources, canals have been dug through the marshes. When a storm strikes, the canals carry seawater farther into the marshes than it would normally flow. The saltwater kills plants and animals. The plants that once grew in the marshes die, and the marshes become ponds. Fortunately, the Wetlands Conservation and Restoration Fund was established in 1989 to create programs that will save and protect Louisiana's coastline.[3]

▲ The Atchafalaya Basin is a large area of swampy wetlands. Cajun fishermen depend on the basin and the river for food and recreation.

▶ The Mighty Mississippi and Ohio Rivers

The Mississippi River is one of the greatest rivers in the world. It flows in a southerly direction to the Gulf of Mexico, as do all the rivers in the state of Louisiana. If they do not actually flow into the Gulf, they flow into rivers that do. The lowermost part of the Mississippi River lies entirely within Louisiana. Other main rivers are the Red, Ouachita, Sabine, Pearl, Atchafalaya, and Calcasieu.

Rivers are not the only water source in Louisiana. Lakes are found in low-lying regions. The largest lake, Lake Pontchartrain, covers 625 square miles. It is a lake that has both seawater and freshwater. This type of lake is referred to as a brackish lake. Louisiana has other brackish lakes as well, including Salvador, Sabine, White, Grand, Calcasieu, and Caillou lakes. Many of the freshwater lakes are on the Red River and its tributaries.

Water plays an essential role in the economy as well as the wildlife and landscape of Louisiana.

Economy

No state could ask for a better location than Louisiana. Because the Mississippi River links other states such as Iowa and Kansas and the Arkansas farmlands to the north, many states' products come together in Louisiana. Barges of grain from the Midwest float down rivers that connect to the Mississippi and ultimately to Louisiana's ports. The state has a huge shipping industry, exporting billions of dollars worth of products each year. Even in earlier times, American Indians used the Mississippi River to trade with other tribes. Today, the Port of New Orleans has over twenty miles of loading and unloading facilities. Thousands of vessels dock here each year, loading and unloading cargo from around the world.

Louisiana's workforce in 2001 was almost 2.1 million. Thirty-eight percent were employed in the service industry. Twenty four percent worked in the wholesale or retail trade.

Louisiana's sugarcane industry ▶ skyrocketed in 1751 and grew steadily until the Civil War, when production came to a halt. It returned in the late 1800s and is still strong.

In the eighteenth century, cotton and sugarcane drove the Louisiana economy. By the nineteenth century, wood and timber became essential and by the twentieth century, the discovery of petroleum and natural gas helped strengthen the state's economy. At the turn of the twenty-first century, commerce, mining, manufacturing, and tourism drove Louisiana's economy.

▶ Petroleum

A prospector discovered oil in Jennings, Louisiana, in 1901. More wells sprang up, and over the next few decades, prospectors would mine oil, gas, and chemicals from the earth. Since then, the petrochemical industry has become the heart of Louisiana's economy. The state contains just under 10 percent of all known United States oil reserves and is the country's third-largest producer of petroleum.[1] Louisiana is also a large supplier of natural gas and produces more than one quarter of all United States supplies.

Louisiana petroleum refineries produce enough gas to fill 800 million automobile gas tanks.[2] The state's sixteen refineries include one of the four largest in the Western Hemisphere. Louisiana refineries also produce jet fuels, lubricants, and some six hundred other products made from petroleum.

Laws regarding mining are not strict in Louisiana. That leniency is good for the economy, but not good for the environment. With the constant drilling and erosion of the earth, taking valuable minerals and deposits, not much will be left in the areas around the mines and oil wells. In addition, the threat of oil spills in the Gulf of Mexico and water contamination remains high.

▶ Shipbuilding

Louisiana is a leader in shipbuilding. The largest private employer in Louisiana during the 1990s was Avondale Shipyards. The company built minesweepers, transports, and tankers and employed over five thousand people. It is one of the world's largest shipbuilders and builds many of the United States Navy's ships.

Some of the United States' leading ports are located in Louisiana. Based on the amount of tonnage each port handles, Port of South Louisiana between New Orleans and Baton Rouge is at the top of the list. This port handles 185 million tons of cargo each year. It is enormous. It covers 205 acres. The Globalplex Intermodal Terminal moves everything from steel to natural gas. Baton Rouge's port ranks fourth in the United States in tonnage. It moves

▲ *Huge cargo ships like the one pictured are built in Louisiana's shipyards.*

86 million tons of cargo every year. Port of Lake Charles comes in twelfth.

Louisiana Industries

Other industries thrive in Louisiana. Chemical production is the leading manufacturing activity in this state. Louisiana produces crude oil, sugar, salt, natural gas, and sulphur. Many manufacturing companies are located along the Mississippi River from Baton Rouge to New Orleans. Other industries include paper production, food processing plants, and petroleum refining. Lumber products and wood, fabricated metals, and electrical equipment are also made there. Louisiana has links to other countries, many in Europe and South America, and encourages foreign trade.

Natural Resources

Because of the abundance of water, Louisiana has many natural resources. Farming is an important industry in Louisiana. The five leading farm crops are cotton, sugarcane, soybeans, rice, and corn. In the northern part of the state, farmers grow oats, peaches, strawberries, and alfalfa while smaller farms produce a wider assortment of vegetables and fruit. Rice and cotton are grown close to the Mississippi River. These water-loving crops grow along the Red and Calcasieu rivers. Farmers also grow rice along the southwest Gulf Coast. Rice is a staple food in Louisiana cooking.

Pierre Emmanuel Prudhomme introduced cotton to Louisiana in 1718. He had a large plantation, but cotton was not commonly grown until the invention of the cotton gin in 1793. Two hundred years later, cotton is still an important part of Louisiana's economy. In 1997, Louisiana ranked sixth in the United States in cotton production.

Farming is an important industry in Louisiana. Crops accounted for 64 percent of Louisiana's farm income in 2000. Livestock like cattle and chickens accounted for 36 percent of the state's income.

Fish and Forests

Fish are another important part of Louisiana's economy. The value of catch in 2000 was $419 million, the second largest in the country after Alaska. Shrimp are the most profitable catch and are exported globally. Menhaden is a fish raised specifically for livestock and fertilizer and ranks second in value. Other seafood caught are oysters, blue crab, and tuna. Louisiana is known for its crayfish. They are raised inland in fish-farming operations.

Surprisingly, Louisiana is one of the leading lumber producers in the country. Concerns over lumbering practices

▲ Louisiana's shrimp industry accounts for 85 percent of the state's edible fishery production.

in the northwestern part of the United States increased Louisiana's production of lumber. Most of the forests in the state are privately owned. Wood is harvested to make plywood, furniture, pulp and paper, and fuel. Spanish moss is collected, dried, and used as packaging material.

Mining

Salt is mined in Louisiana. It comes from large salt mines found in the Gulf of Mexico. One of the largest salt mines in the world is found on Avery Island, Louisiana. It is also the oldest. Some of these mines are a mile across and up to fifty thousand feet deep and produce almost 100 percent pure rock salt. The first sulphur mined in America came from Louisiana, and the state is still a principal producer of the mineral.[3]

▲ *This archival photograph from the 1940s shows a barge filled with sulphur traveling down the channel from Port Sulphur, Louisiana.*

▶ **Tourism**

Hundreds of thousands of people visit Louisiana each year. People come from all over the world to enjoy the culture, sights, and sounds of this interesting state. Though many come to see the state parks and national forests, most come to see the bustling city of New Orleans. There are five travel regions in Louisiana that attract people. They include Sportsman's Paradise, Crossroads, Cajun Country, Plantation Country, and the Greater New Orleans Area.

Sportsman's Paradise refers to the northern part of Louisiana. Fishing and hunting are the favorite activities here. This region is quickly growing as parks, museums, theme parks, and sporting events open every year.

Crossroads is located in the central part of Louisiana. It is pretty country with Victorian homes, white picket fences, antique shops, lakes abundant with fish, rugged frontier towns, and historical buildings.

Cajun Country is at the southern end of Louisiana. Cajuns, where this area gets its name, were first known as Acadians when they immigrated to Canada. Then they were driven out of Canada and found a home in Louisiana. The Cajun people are known for their hospitality and good food.

Plantation Country lies to the east of Cajun Country and before the New Orleans region. The Mississippi River flows through this area. Vast tracts of land with enormous mansions are located beside the river. This is where wealthy farmers raised large crops of cotton, soybeans, and sugarcane. Tourists visit Plantation Country not only to see the magnificent buildings, but also to hear the histories of the people who lived here.

Government

As in other states, Louisiana's government structure includes the executive, legislative, and judicial branches. Since its acceptance into statehood in April 1812, Louisiana has had eleven constitutions. Baton Rouge is the state capital.

▶ Branches of Government

The executive branch consists of the governor, lieutenant governor, secretary of state, attorney general, state treasurer, and the commissioners of agriculture, insurance, and elections. These are elected officials, and each serves for four years.

The first governor of Louisiana was William Charles Cole Claiborne. He became governor when Louisiana was a territory. On December 30, 1803, after the Louisiana Purchase, Claiborne relieved French authorities of their responsibilities in Louisiana. He was also governor when Louisiana became a state, and he served until 1816.

The state's legislative branch consists of a 39-member senate and a 105-member house of representatives. Officials are elected for four-year terms. Even before it became a state, Louisiana had a house of representatives and a legislative council.

The judicial branch has a supreme court, court of appeals, district courts, and other lesser courts. The supreme court has a chief justice and seven associate judges. They are elected for ten-year terms. Most states base their judicial system on English common law. Louisiana is different.

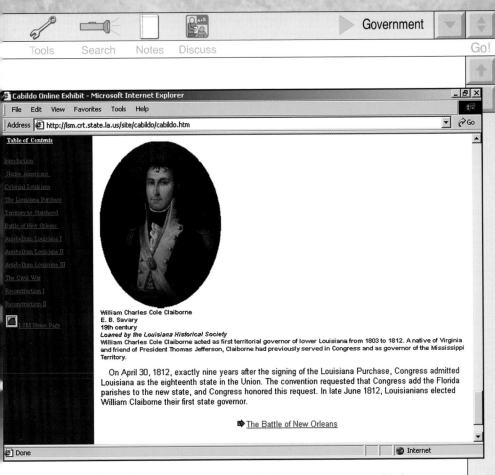

Cabildo Online Exhibit - Microsoft Internet Explorer
File   Edit   View   Favorites   Tools   Help
Address   http://lsm.crt.state.la.us/site/cabildo/cabildo.htm   Go

William Charles Cole Claiborne
E. B. Savary
19th century
Loaned by the Louisiana Historical Society
William Charles Cole Claiborne acted as first territorial governor of lower Louisiana from 1803 to 1812. A native of Virginia and friend of President Thomas Jefferson, Claiborne had previously served in Congress and as governor of the Mississippi Territory.

On April 30, 1812, exactly nine years after the signing of the Louisiana Purchase, Congress admitted Louisiana as the eighteenth state in the Union. The convention requested that Congress add the Florida parishes to the new state, and Congress honored this request. In late June 1812, Louisianians elected William Claiborne their first state governor.

➡ The Battle of New Orleans

Done   Internet

▲ *William Charles Cole Claiborne was the territorial governor of Orleans in 1803. From 1812 until 1816, he served as the first elected governor of Louisiana.*

Under the common law system, a judicial decision depends on previous courts' decisions and on the citizens' customs. In Louisiana, judges decide cases by a strict set of rules or a code of law. Over time, however, the Code Napoléon has been changed to reflect the English common law followed by other states. Code Napoléon was enacted in 1807 and is based on the Code Civil de Français, still used today in France. It is named for the French emperor Napoléon Bonaparte, who also helped to create this set of rules. Because Louisiana was a part of the Napoleonic conquest, the code was introduced here.[1]

Federal Representation

Louisiana voters elect seven members to the House of Representatives and two members to the Senate. In presidential elections, the state casts nine electoral votes.

Local Government: Louisiana's Parishes

What are known as counties in most states are called parishes in Louisiana. The word *parish* is a term for administrative areas of the Roman Catholic Church. When the state was a Spanish colony in the eighteenth century, parishes were formed for religious administration. The constitution of 1845 started the parish system, and today there are sixty-four parishes in Louisiana. These parishes provide local services including road repairs and police protection. Many parishes have a "police jury" that acts like a county board of commissioners. Parish officials are elected for four-year terms. Some parishes have a mayor and city-parish council form of local government.

Political Leaders From Louisiana

Well-known Louisianan leaders include the state's most famous governor, Huey Long. Nicknamed the Kingfish, he promised to tax oil and logging companies and to spend the money to help the state's poor people. He was elected in 1928 and hired people who were loyal to him. Long became a senator in 1930 and even planned to run for president, but he was assassinated in 1935.[2]

Mary Landrieu is a well-known senator from Louisiana. Born in Baton Rouge, she is the daughter of Moon Landrieu, a former mayor of New Orleans. Mary Landrieu served as a state representative from 1979 to 1987 and was state treasurer from 1987 to 1995.

In 1996 she won election to the U.S. Senate and was reelected in 2002.

Although the African-American population in Louisiana is less than the white population, many African Americans have risen to power. Kermit A. Parker, a pharmacist, ran for governor in 1952 and became the first African American to seek any state office since before the 1900s. He did not win, but he did open the doors for other African Americans like Ernest "Dutch" Morial to pursue political opportunities. Morial became the first African American in the state legislature since the end of the Civil War. He was also elected a two-term mayor of New Orleans from 1978 to 1986.

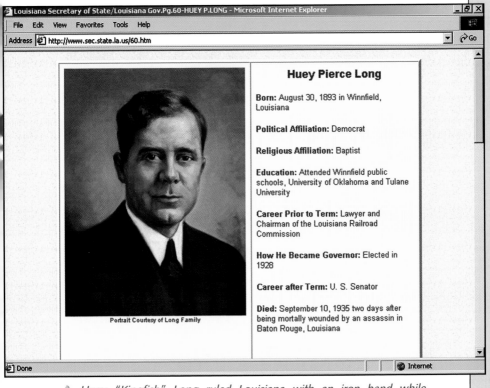

Louisiana Secretary of State/Louisiana Gov.Pg.60-HUEY P.LONG - Microsoft Internet Explorer

File　Edit　View　Favorites　Tools　Help

Address　http://www.sec.state.la.us/60.htm

Huey Pierce Long

Born: August 30, 1893 in Winnfield, Louisiana

Political Affiliation: Democrat

Religious Affiliation: Baptist

Education: Attended Winnfield public schools, University of Oklahoma and Tulane University

Career Prior to Term: Lawyer and Chairman of the Louisiana Railroad Commission

How He Became Governor: Elected in 1928

Career after Term: U. S. Senator

Died: September 10, 1935 two days after being mortally wounded by an assassin in Baton Rouge, Louisiana

Portrait Courtesy of Long Family

Done　　　　　　　　　　　　　　　　　Internet

Huey "Kingfish" Long ruled Louisiana with an iron hand while governor. While the state prospered financially during his tenure, corruption was widespread.

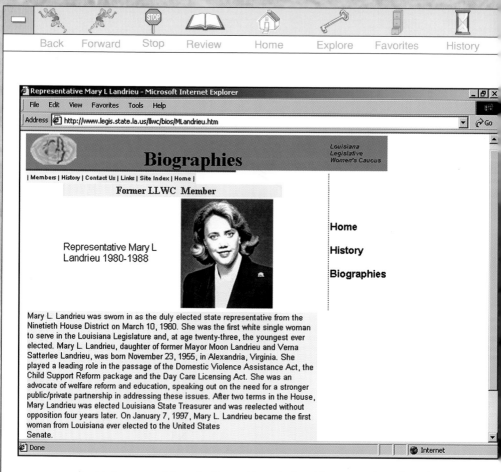

Representative Mary L Landrieu - Microsoft Internet Explorer

File   Edit   View   Favorites   Tools   Help

Address http://www.legis.state.la.us/llwc/bios/MLandrieu.htm

Biographies

Louisiana Legislative Women's Caucus

| Members | History | Contact Us | Links | Site Index | Home |

Former LLWC Member

Representative Mary L Landrieu 1980-1988

Home

History

Biographies

Mary L. Landrieu was sworn in as the duly elected state representative from the Ninetieth House District on March 10, 1980. She was the first white single woman to serve in the Louisiana Legislature and, at age twenty-three, the youngest ever elected. Mary L. Landrieu, daughter of former Mayor Moon Landrieu and Verna Satterlee Landrieu, was born November 23, 1955, in Alexandria, Virginia. She played a leading role in the passage of the Domestic Violence Assistance Act, the Child Support Reform package and the Day Care Licensing Act. She was an advocate of welfare reform and education, speaking out on the need for a stronger public/private partnership in addressing these issues. After two terms in the House, Mary Landrieu was elected Louisiana State Treasurer and was reelected without opposition four years later. On January 7, 1997, Mary L. Landrieu became the first woman from Louisiana ever elected to the United States Senate.

Done   Internet

▲ *At the age of twenty-three, Mary L. Landrieu was elected to the Louisiana legislature. She now serves as the first female U.S. senator from Louisiana.*

▶ Drugs and Crime

Illegal drugs are a huge problem in Louisiana. Because of the many ports and harbors, it is easier to smuggle drugs through Louisiana than other states. Violent crime is also a problem in New Orleans and other big cities. It is believed that illegal drugs are the main reason for the high crime and murder rates in Louisiana. In violent crime, Louisiana was ranked in 2000 with the seventh highest occurrence among the states. Also in the year 2000,

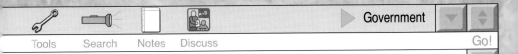
Louisiana had 12.5 murders per 100,000 people, the highest rate for murder.[3] Despite these statistics, violent crime rates have come down in recent years.

Health and Education

Louisiana faces other problems including its health and welfare system and education. This state has the lowest income tax rates in the country, and citizens do not have to pay property taxes. While this may sound good to many people, less money is coming into the state and local governments to pay for programs and schools. Louisiana has one of the highest percentages of children living in poverty as well as the highest rate of infant mortality. The general health of its people is low compared to that of other states.

The state's educational system has also performed poorly. According to the Measure Up 2002 program, a state-by-state report card for schools, most of Louisiana's schools are academically below average.[4] School boards, teachers, and parents have vowed to make changes in the way they educate their children.

History

When the first European explorers came to the Louisiana area, they were in search of gold. Long before they arrived, American Indians lived in the area. They can be traced back to 700 B.C. Mounds are still found where ancient villages once flourished. The mounds are between fifty and two hundred feet in length and anywhere from five to fifty feet in height. These are both ceremonial mounds

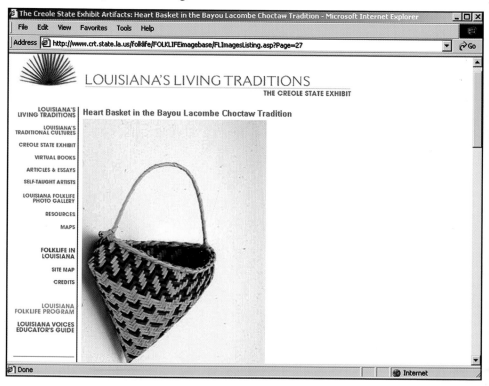

The Creole State Exhibit Artifacts: Heart Basket in the Bayou Lacombe Choctaw Tradition - Microsoft Internet Explorer

File   Edit   View   Favorites   Tools   Help

Address http://www.crt.state.la.us/folklife/FOLKLIFEimagebase/FLImagesListing.asp?Page=27   Go

LOUISIANA'S LIVING TRADITIONS
THE CREOLE STATE EXHIBIT

LOUISIANA'S LIVING TRADITIONS

LOUISIANA'S TRADITIONAL CULTURES

CREOLE STATE EXHIBIT

VIRTUAL BOOKS

ARTICLES & ESSAYS

SELF-TAUGHT ARTISTS

LOUISIANA FOLKLIFE PHOTO GALLERY

RESOURCES

MAPS

FOLKLIFE IN LOUISIANA

SITE MAP

CREDITS

LOUISIANA FOLKLIFE PROGRAM

LOUISIANA VOICES EDUCATOR'S GUIDE

Heart Basket in the Bayou Lacombe Choctaw Tradition

Done   Internet

▲ Baskets such as this one were made by the Choctaw, Chitimacha, and Koasati tribes. This basket was made out of split river cane and may have been used for processing salt or storing dried herbs.

and burial mounds. Many artifacts such as arrowheads and pottery have been found in the mounds. Archaeologists think that mounds found at a site called Watson Brake near Monroe, in northeast Louisiana, may be the oldest known remnants of human construction in North America at five thousand years old.

When Spanish explorers first discovered the area we know today as Louisiana, three American Indian groups lived there: the Caddoan, Muskogean, and Tunican people. Caddoan people included the Caddo, Natchitoches, Yatasi, and Adai. They lived in the northwestern part of Louisiana. The Muskogean people, the Houma, Choctaw, Acolapissa, and Taensa, lived in east central Louisiana near the Mississippi River. Most of the Tunicans, including the Chitimacha, Atakapa, and several smaller groups, lived along the Gulf Coast.[1] As more Europeans moved into the region, these American Indians moved out, died in war or from disease, or intermarried with the Europeans.

The Chitimacha tribe has lived in the area for centuries. When the Acadians, French-speaking people from Canada, arrived in 1764, the two cultures merged through marriage. There is still a Chitimacha reservation in the state, which is home to nearly two hundred people.

Arrival of the Spanish

Spaniard Hernando de Soto, with his expedition, was one of the first explorers to reach Louisiana. He led his soldiers through Arkansas into Louisiana in 1541 and 1542. With those soldiers came disease. Because American Indians did not have immunity to the diseases, many of them died, and sometimes entire tribes were wiped out. Once de Soto left, few Europeans ventured into Louisiana for nearly 150 years.

French Rule

In 1682, French explorer René-Robert Cavelier, Sieur de La Salle, claimed the Mississippi River valley for France. Louisiana was now under French rule, and France built forts along the Gulf of Mexico including parts of Alabama. Natchitoches, founded in 1714, was the first permanent white settlement in Louisiana. Nouvelle-Orléans, another early French settlement, was established in 1718 to secure the lower Mississippi against France's rival colonial powers, Spain and Great Britain. In 1722, New Orleans became the colony's capital. Louisiana remained a French colony until the early 1760s.

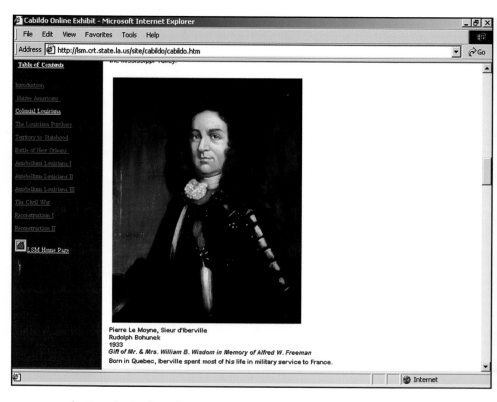

Cabildo Online Exhibit - Microsoft Internet Explorer

File   Edit   View   Favorites   Tools   Help

Address http://lsm.crt.state.la.us/site/cabildo/cabildo.htm

Pierre Le Moyne, Sieur d'Iberville
Rudolph Bohunek
1933
Gift of Mr. & Mrs. William B. Wisdom in Memory of Alfred W. Freeman
Born in Quebec, Iberville spent most of his life in military service to France.

Internet

Born in Quebec, Pierre Le Moyne, Sieur d'Iberville, founded the city of New Orleans in 1718.

In 1762, France gave Spain the Louisiana colony in a secret treaty called the Treaty of Fontainebleau. The local French citizens, called Creoles, were not happy with Spanish rule. Many rebelled, but Spain remained in control.

In the 1760s, many people migrated to Louisiana from Europe. They also came from what is now Nova Scotia, Canada, but was then called Acadia. Four thousand French settlers known as Acadians arrived in Louisiana, driven from their homes by the British victory in the French and Indian War.

When Napoléon Bonaparte became the emperor of France, Spain was a weakened country. He convinced Spain to give Louisiana back to France in another secret treaty called the Treaty of San Ildefonso in 1800. In 1803, France sold the Louisiana Territory to the United States for $15 million.[2] This huge piece of land consisted not only of Louisiana, but also most of western North America from Canada to the Gulf of Mexico. It was called the Louisiana Purchase and nearly doubled the size of the United States. In 1804, the territory was divided into two parts.

The census in 1810 showed that the southern part of the territory, known as the Territory of Orleans, had enough people to become one of the states of the United States of America. At that time, seventy-six thousand people lived in Louisiana. In 1811, a state constitution was drawn up, and on April 30, 1812, Louisiana became the eighteenth state.

War Rages in Louisiana

As soon as Louisiana became part of the Union, it joined the war against Great Britain, the War of 1812. Even though a peace treaty (the Treaty of Ghent) had been signed between Britain and the United States in 1814, the

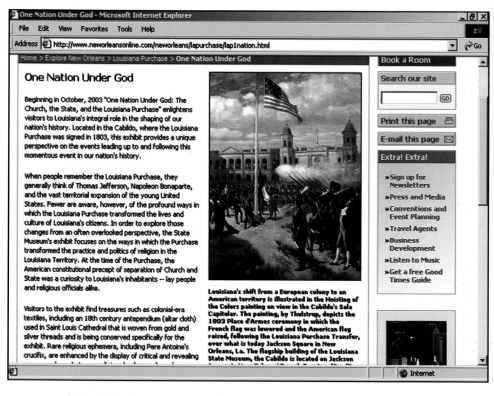

> In 1803, the Louisiana Purchase nearly doubled the size of the United States. The state of Louisiana as well as twelve other states or parts of states were created from the territory purchased from France.

people of Louisiana were some of the last to know. This happened because Louisiana was so far from the North and the East Coast. The Battle of New Orleans was fought after the treaty was signed. Most of the Americans were led by Tennessean Andrew Jackson. Many British soldiers died but only seventy-one Americans died.

After the War of 1812, business boomed in Louisiana. The steamboat replaced keelboats, making the transportation of people and cargo faster and easier. Steamboats could carry large amounts of cargo up and down the Mississippi River in just a few short days. By 1840, New

Orleans became the fourth largest city in the United States and the second largest port after New York. Farmers from other states moved to Louisiana for its rich soil. The Caddo Indians sold much of their land to the farmers.

The Civil War and Aftermath

On January 26, 1861, Louisiana seceded from the Union and six weeks later joined the Confederate States of America.[3] Louisiana's leaders felt that their state government was better equipped to handle the state's problems than the federal government was. Slavery also played a large role in the secession. Plantation owners believed they needed slave labor to keep their farming industries alive and profitable.

In 1862 the Union Navy and then the Army invaded New Orleans. They remained there until the end of the war. Admiral David G. Farragut not only captured New Orleans but also other ports along the Mississippi River. In 1865, after the end of the war, the Thirteenth Amendment was ratified, officially freeing all American slaves.

In 1868, Louisiana was readmitted to the Union but life there was nothing like it had been before the war. After the Civil War, Louisiana was devastated financially. Plantations that once relied on slave labor could no longer survive without them.

Struggles and Promise

The new freedom many African Americans were given did not come easy. White supremacist groups such as the Ku Klux Klan and the White League terrorized African Americans and any whites who supported the African-American community. In the early twentieth century, Louisiana began to grow and change. With the discovery

of oil, there was promise for a better quality of life for all the people of Louisiana. World War II encouraged oil production. With the increase in wealth, more people moved from farms to the cities. Still, blacks were segregated from whites in many areas. They had separate drinking fountains, buses, bathrooms, and schools. Along with other southern states, Louisiana slowly began to integrate African-American children into white schools.

It would be many years later before the African-American community in Louisiana would have the same privileges as whites. In 1977, the first African-American mayor was elected in New Orleans. His name was Ernest "Dutch" Morial. By the twenty-first century, hundreds of African Americans were serving in public office in the state. Louisiana still has work to do in race relations, but progress is being made.

Today, Louisiana is a state committed to economic growth, better education, and improved health care for its people. A state rich in history, Louisiana has come a long way since its beginnings. It is still the state of snowy cotton, sweet magnolias, old mossy oak trees, and planta-tions.[4] To many, Louisiana is the sweetest state of all.

David Glasgow Farragut's success at Mobile Bay and New Orleans secured his rank as First Admiral of the U.S. Navy in 1866.

Chapter Notes

Chapter 1. The Pelican State

1. Office of Coastal Restoration and Management, "Coast 2050: A Partnership," *Louisiana Department of Natural Resources,* November 8, 2000, <http://www.dnr.state.la.us/crm/2050.ssi> (May 2, 2003).

Chapter 2. Land and Climate

1. "Personal Accounts of Hurricane Audrey: Thursday June 27, 1957," *Local Stats,* n.d. <http://members.tripod.com/~marshmom/susan.html> (May 2, 2003).

2. Office of Coastal Restoration and Management, "Coast 2050: A Partnership," *Louisiana Department of Natural Resources,* November 8, 2000, <http://www.dnr.state.la.us/crm/2050.ssi> (May 2, 2003).

3. America's Wetland, "Campaign to Save Coastal Louisiana," n.d., <http://www.americaswetland.com> (May 1, 2003).

Chapter 3. Economy

1. Louisiana Department of Economic Development and the Department of Culture, Recreation, and Tourism, *Louisiana Economy,* December 12, 1994, <http://www.crt.state.la.us/crt/profiles/economy.htm> (May 1, 2003).

2. Ibid.

3. "History of Salt," *Salt Institute,* n.d., <http://www.saltinstitute.org/38.html> (May 1, 2003).

Chapter 4. Government

1. Louisiana State Museum, "The Cabildo Exihibit: The Louisiana Purchase," n.d., <http://lsm.crt.state.la.us/cabildo/cab4 .htm) (May 1, 2003).

2. Harry T. Williams, *Huey Long* (New York: Alfred A Knopf, 1970), pp. 312–313, 552–553.

3. U.S. Department of Justice, "State Crime Data," *Bureau of Justice Statistics,* November 14, 2001, <http://www.ojp.usdoj.gov/bjs/data/stateucr/ucrla.wk1> (May 1, 2003).

4. The National Center for Public Policy and Higher Education, "States At A Glance: Louisiana," *Measuring Up 2002*, n.d., <http://measuringup.highereducation.org/2002/stateglance.cfm> (May 1, 2003).

Chapter 5. History

1. William B. Glover, "A History of the Caddo Indians," *The Louisiana Historical Quarterly*, vol. 18., no. 4. October 1935, <http://www.salsburg.com/Indians.html> (May 1, 2003).

2. National Archives and Records Administration, "American Originals," *Louisiana Purchase Treaty, 1803*, n.d., <http://www.archives.gov/exhibit_hall/american_originals_iv/sections/louisiana_purchase_treaty.html> (May 30, 2003).

3. Louisiana State Museum, "The Cabildo Exihibit: The Louisiana Purchase," n.d., <http://lsm.crt.state.la.us/cabildo/cab4.htm> (May 1, 2003).

4. Doraline Fontane, state song "Give Me Louisiana."

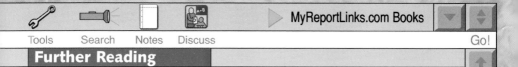
Further Reading

Burgan, Michael. *The Louisiana Purchase*. Mankato, Minn.: Compass Point Books, 2002.

Capstone Press Staff. *Louisiana*. Minnetonka, Minn.: Capstone Press, Incorporated, 2003.

Culbertson, Manie. *Louisiana: The Land and Its People Student Skillbuilder*. Pelican Publishing Company, 1999.

Dartez, Cecilia Casrill. *L Is For Louisiana*. Gretna, La.: Pelican Publishing Company, 2002.

Gravelle, Karen, and Sylviane Diouf. *Growing Up in Crawfish Country: A Cajun Childhood*. Danbury, Conn.: Franklin Watts, 1998.

Hintz, Martin. *Louisiana*. Danbury, Conn.: Children's Press, 1998.

Johnstone, Robb. *A Guide to Louisiana*. Mankato, Minn.: Weigl Publishers, 2000.

Kavanagh, James. *Louisiana Birds*. Blaine, Wash.: Waterford Press, Limited, 1999.

LeVert, Suzanne. *Louisiana*. Tarrytown, N.Y.: Marshall Cavendish, Inc., 1997.

Thompson, Kathleen. *Louisiana*. Austin, Tex.: Raintree Steck-Vaughn Publishers, 1996.

Vidrine, Beverly B. *A Mardi Gras Dictionary*. Gretna, La.: Pelican Publishing Company, 1997.